Alex DèLarge

Tuesday Girl

Naughty Shorts

Facebook/NortyShorts

TUESDAY GIRL

Written by

Alex DèLarge

Blue **B**unny.**A**gency
London

Chapters

1. The Train...
2. Contact...
3. The gift...
4. Showtime...
5. The money shot...
6. The doorbell...

Alex DèLarge

Copyright

TUESDAY GIRL

Adult short stories in the series "Naughty Shorts"

First Published April 2016

All rights reserved.

ISBN: 978-0-9934180-3-7

This edition published in April 2016
by The Blue Bunny Agency
Facebook.com/BlueBunnyAgency

Illustrations by Dreamstime.com

© **The Blue Bunny.Agency**

Dedication

To Marion…

…for always believing in me.

Preface

"Tuesday Girl" is a funny and sexy adult bed-time story!

This is the second book in the series..."Naughty Shorts".

Are you sitting comfortably?

Are you dressed appropriately…?!

…then let's begin!

Chapter 1 – The train...

Alex didn't enjoy his monthly trips to the City. Even though he travelled 1st class, to pretty much guarantee a seat, the journey was uncomfortable and boring. Today, though, he remembered to take his headphones, to listen to music and chill out.

On the return journey, the train filled up with commuters, returning home.

Half dozing, Alex noticed a well dressed gent sit beside him.

Stowing his bag, in the overhead tray, his cell

phone fell out of his bag, onto Alex's head, bouncing on the seat beside him.

"So sorry...", the gent said sheepishly, taking his seat.

The smooth Jazz, from Alex's headphones allowed Alex to gently drift off to sleep.

Alex's station was pretty much at the 'end of the line'. By then, the carriage was empty, except for the bag above his head.

If I left something on the train, I'd like someone to try and return it to me, thought Alex, taking the bag from the rack and leaving the train.

Chapter 2 – Contact…

Now at home, searching the bag for clues to the owner's identity, Alex found a business card, in a signed hardback book.

A 'phone call and a meetup later, Alex returned the bag.

"I'll send you something to say thanks…", said the gent "…just email me your address".

"Sure" replied Alex, that signed book must have meant something to him.

Chapter 3 – The gift...

It was Tuesday – Alex never got the hang of Tuesdays...not the start of the week, nor quite mid-week...he felt bored and drowsy, at his workstation, working from home never came easy for Alex.

A ring at the doorbell, brought Alex to his feet...

"Aha, my online order has arrived!", he announced to himself.

Snatching the door open, Alex was confronted with, not the usual courier guy, but a slim, stunningly attractive, young Asian woman.

"Your Alex, right?"..."Can I come in...Dave sent me", she purred, brushing past him.

"Dave...who's Dave?", said Alex, now transfixed on his new guest's pert bottom, wiggling into his lounge.

...then Alex got it...Dave was the lost luggage guy.

The woman had already made herself comfortable on his couch, crossing her legs, showing a hint of creamy thigh, above her Black stockings.

Stockings, my favorite! thought Alex.

"Nice place, Alex...got any Red wine?"

"Cab Sav coming up", offered Alex, feeling happier by the minute!

"I didn't get your name", asked Alex, finishing up his second glass. "I didn't give it..." she replied, with a saucy smile

"...but you can call me 'Tuesday'"

"...and it's about time we got started...Dave told me to show how very, very grateful he is to you...", Tuesday added, seductively.

"...I'm going to need some help, so I'm going to call a friend."

"What kind of help, Tuesday?", Alex asked.

"The kind any man wants...why have one woman, when you can take two?"

"He's ready, come on in" Tuesday said down her cell 'phone.

"Lead me to the bedroom, now", Tuesday commanded.

Chapter 4 – Showtime...

Alex was half way up the stairs, when a ring of the doorbell resulted in Tuesday letting in another drop-dead gorgeous specimen of voluptuous womanhood.

"Showtime!" announced Tuesday, to her friend, as they both followed Alex up the stairs.

Now in the bedroom, Alex turned to find both women stripping down the most sexy, matching, Black, lacy baby-dolls...with those silky, sensuous, stockings framing their g-string panties.

"Has the Viagra kicked in yet, Alex?", said Tuesday 2.

"I don't take Viagra", replied Alex…

"Well, I can see *someone* disagrees", insisted Tuesday, gesturing to his pants.

Sure enough, Alex was ready…

"Let's lose the clothes, Alex, you're overdressed for this party"

I've never had my shirt ripped off, thought Alex, as buttons pinged onto the floor, along with every stitch of clothes from his body.

"Much better"

Tuesday was clearly satisfied with her handiwork, as she swung her legs around his waist and one arm around his neck, in one fluid move.

Her free hand guided Alex's cock, parting her pussy lips. She slowly and gently lowered her bottom onto him.

Alex felt himself slide deep inside her – what a wonderful feeling.

"Move your ass!", said Tuesday 2, shoving them both onto the bed.

"You bitch...", Tuesday gasped, "...you know that makes me cum"...now astride Alex, gently rotating her hips.

Tuesday was right, Alex could feel her spasms, tightening and relaxing around him.

"My turn" demanded Tuesday 2, discarding her panties and shoving her pussy inches from his mouth. Do you think you can focus less on hers and more on mine?... "

"...get your tongue working, Alex"

What a sight…Tuesday 2's pussy was piece of art - shaven save Heart shaped, manicured, Black hair, just above her clit.

Her moist lips invoked memory of hints and tips, from a top shelf magazine article.

….he set about licking her like a lollypop…his tongue circling around her inner lips, then exploring inside her.

Tuesday 2 was making gentle sounds, in time with encouraging thrusts of her hips…Alex now settling on sucking on her clit.

Tuesday, now recovered, was grinding on Alex like a crazed cowgirl, clearly working on her second orgasm.

These women are like a tag team, thought Alex, If only I had cameras in this place – the action replays would be…well, awesome!

…then he felt both of the women explode in synchronized pleasure.

Alex was enjoying the taste of Tuesday 2's juices, as he gently pushed his tongue inside - her pussy still pulsating.

Chapter 5 – The money shot...

"Come on partner..." gasped Tuesday, dismounting, "...time to give Alex his fun".

Tuesday and Tuesday 2 took turns to lick Alex's cock (they must have read the same top-shelf magazine!).

"Hmm...feels like it's 'Money Shot' time, Alex", Tuesday concluded.

"In the pussy or on our tits?", she asked.

"Pussy", Alex decided, as he took Tuesday 2, doggie style, across the bed.

Taking a handful of her long hair in one hand and gripping her hip with the other, he pushed inside her with aggression he didn't know he possessed.

"WOW" Tuesday 2 cried, as Alex collapsed beside her. "I think you filled me up with the mother lode!".

"And finger-licking good!" Tuesday added, tasting his cum, from Tuesday 2's dripping pussy.

Chapter 6 – The doorbell...

The doorbell?....seriously?...not now!

Rubbing the sleep from his eyes, Alex woke from his snooze, at his workstation. No, this couldn't have been a dream?, Alex thought, in pure disbelief!

It was a courier at the door – a young Asian girl...!

"Is this your last job?...", asked Alex, "...as I think I'd like to share what's in your box!"

"As a matter of fact, it is" she replied, brushing past him "Why don't we open my box, now!", she purred, playfully.

"Care to give me a hand?"

Yep, I think I'm getting the hang of Tuesdays…

…thanks Dave!

The End

NaughtyShorts

Also by Alex DèLarge

"The Waitress"

…and coming soon…

"Sharpen my Pencil"

"The Simple French Tart"

"Pet shop Pussy"

Like us on Facebook

NortyShorts.com

www.ingramcontent.com/pod-product-compliance
Lightning Source LLC
Chambersburg PA
CBHW041820040426
42452CB00004B/163